Animal Communication

Phil Gates

St. Mary's Primary School
Link Lane
Pulborough
W. Sussex RH20 2AN

CAMBRIDGE UNIVERSITY PRESS

Cambridge Reading

General Editors
Richard Brown and Kate Ruttle

Consultant Editor
Jean Glasberg

PUBLISHED BY THE PRESS SYNDICATE OF THE UNIVERSITY OF CAMBRIDGE
The Pitt Building, Trumpington Street, Cambridge CB2 1RP, United Kingdom

CAMBRIDGE UNIVERSITY PRESS
The Edinburgh Building, Cambridge CB2 2RU, United Kingdom
40 West 20th Street, New York, NY 10011-4211, USA
10 Stamford Road, Oakleigh, Melbourne 3166, Australia

Text © Phil Gates 1997
Illustrations © Tony Kenyon 1997; © Toni Hargreaves 1997 (p.7, *top*; p.23, *top*)

This book is in copyright. Subject to statutory exception and to the provisions of relevant collective licensing agreements, no reproduction of any part may take place without the written permission of Cambridge University Press.

First published 1997

Printed in the United Kingdom at the University Press, Cambridge

Typeset in Concorde and Franklin Gothic

A catalogue record for this book is available from the British Library

ISBN 0 521 49966 6 paperback

Picture research: Callie Kendall

Acknowledgements
We are grateful to the following for permission to reproduce photographs:

Front cover: Tony Stone Images (photo: © Kim Heacox)

Back cover: Tony Stone Images (photo: © Tim Davis)

Allsport: 9*b*, © Ben Radford

ARDEA: 9*c*, © Wardene Weisser; 19*t*, © François Gohier

H Bradshaw: 5*t*

Michael Brooke: 4*tl*, 4*tr*, 4*b*, 5*c*, 12*t*, 16*tl*, 16*tr*

Bruce Coleman Ltd: 6*t*, © M P L Fogden; 14*t*, © Joseph Van Wormer; 16*c*, © Kim Taylor

P H Dunn: 19*br*

Frank Lane Picture Agency: 12*c*, © W Wisniewski; 13*bl*, © Roger Wilmshurst; 16*b*, © Michael Callan; 20*bl*, © Terry Whittaker

Phil Gates: 15*c*

Life File: 8*b*, © Andrew Ward; 15*b*, © Juliet Highet; 19*bl*, © Caroline Field; 21*b*, © Nigel Shuttleworth

Nigel Luckhurst: 5*b*

Oxford Scientific Films: 1, © Larry Crowhurst; 6*bl*, © Jos Korenromp; 6*br*, © Tim Davis/Photo Researchers Inc.; 8*t*, © Frank Schneidermeyer; 8*cl*, © Tom Ulrich; 8*cr*, © Scott Camazine & Sue Trainor; 9*tl*, © David B Fleetham; 9*tr*, © Max Gibbs; 10*tl*, © Mark Hamblin; 10*tr*, © Hans Reinhard/Okapia; 10*c*, © Raymond Blythe; 11*t*, © Michael Fogden; 11*c*, © K G Vock/Okapia; 12*b*, © Renee Lynn/Photo Researchers Inc.; 13*t*, 13*c*, © Michael Fogden; 13*br*, © Roland Mayr; 14*c*, © G I Bernard; 14*bl*, Mickey Gibson/Animals Animals; 14*br*, © G I Bernard; 15*t*, © Tom Ulrich; 17*t*, © G I Bernard; 17*c*, © Michael Fogden; 17*bl*, © David B Fleetham; 17*br*, © Irvine Cushing; 18, © Scott Camazine; 20*t*, © M P L Fogden; 20*br*, 21*t*, © Raymond Blythe

Royal National Institute of the Deaf: 22, © Jens Storch

Contents

What is communication? 4

Colour 8

Sound 12

Movement and shape 16

Smell 20

Light 21

Use your head! 22

Glossary 23

Index 24

What is communication?

When we send a message to someone we are trying to communicate with them.

People can use words to communicate with each other.

← Talking is a kind of communication . . .

. . . and so is writing. →

People can also communicate in other ways.

Babies cannot talk or write, but they can still communicate.

Sometimes we use our hands and arms to help us communicate.

Our faces can often tell other people what we are feeling.

Try this

Look into a mirror and see how many different faces you can make. Try to look angry or friendly, happy or sad, worried or frightened. Can you draw the different faces that you made?

Animals cannot talk or write but they can communicate with each other in lots of other ways.

Some animals use colour to communicate.

The bright colours of a coral snake warn other animals that it is dangerous.

Some animals use sound or smell.

Birds sing to each other. They use different songs to communicate different things.

A skunk sends out a powerful smell to warn its enemies away.

Other animals communicate by moving or by changing the shape of their bodies.

When a cat is angry, it arches its back and its fur stands on end. This makes the cat look bigger and more frightening.

Brightly coloured feathers, wagging tails, whistles, grunts and croaks are just some of the things that animals use to communicate with each other.

Colour

Colour is important in animal communication.

Many birds show off their colourful feathers to make other birds notice them.

A male peacock spreads out its brilliant tail feathers to attract female peacocks.

In spring, male ducks grow brightly coloured feathers that help them to attract a mate.

People sometimes wear colourful clothes so that other people will look at them.

8

Many animals have special colours or patterns which help them to recognise animals of their own kind.

Different kinds of fish have their own colour patterns. This helps them to stay together when they swim in large shoals.

Over 150 different kinds of butterfly fish live on a coral reef. Each kind has its own special pattern.

Humming-birds hover in front of flowers and drink the sweet liquid, called nectar, that they find inside.
   There are 320 different kinds of humming-bird. Each type has a special pattern of brightly coloured feathers.

In team games, players need to recognise each other quickly, so each team wears different colours.

9

Red is an important colour in animal communication. It often means 'danger'.

A robin puffs out its red breast feathers to warn other robins that it will fight them if they come too close.

The red belly of a male stickleback warns other sticklebacks in the pond to keep away.

Ladybirds are poisonous to birds. If a bird tries to eat one, it will find that the ladybird tastes very bad and will spit it out. The ladybird's bright red colour reminds the bird never to try to eat a ladybird again.

People often use the colour red to warn of danger. Red traffic lights tell cars to stop.

Other bright colours can mean 'danger' too.

← In tropical rainforests there are poisonous frogs. Their bright colours warn other animals that they are dangerous.

A wasp's yellow-and-black stripes warn other animals that it has a dangerous sting. →

← People copy the wasp's danger signal. We paint yellow-and-black stripes on the back of lorries that are carrying dangerous loads.

Try this

Warning signs need to have simple shapes and big letters that are easy to read. They need to be drawn with bright colours that stand out against the background.

Make your own sign that warns people not to go near a dangerous animal in a zoo.

Sound

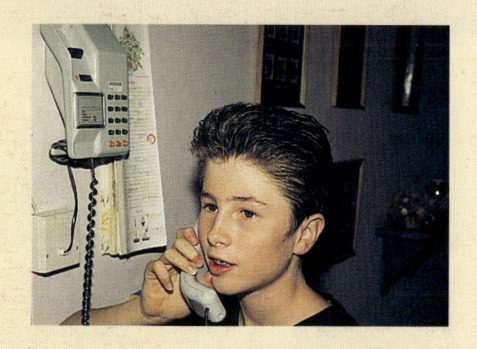

You can recognise your friends by the sound of their voices.

Animals can also recognise each other by the sounds that they make.

Hundreds of seals often live on the same beach. Each seal pup must quickly learn to recognise its mother's call.

When animals live in a group they often call to each other to keep the group together.

Wolves live in packs and they communicate by howling. The sound is carried through the air across great distances. The howl of the wolf-pack leader calls the pack together.

Each kind of animal makes its own sounds. This helps the animals to communicate.

A frog croaks so that other frogs can find it. Each type of frog has its own special croak.

Most birds send messages to each other by singing. Each kind of bird has its own set of songs.

Some animals can make many different sounds. The sounds carry different messages.

Dogs bark loudly and snarl when they want people to keep away from them.

They make short, sharp barks when they are excited and want to play.

They whimper when they are unwell or in pain.

There are many kinds of animals that do not call or sing to each other but still use sound to communicate.

Porcupines have sharp spines called quills on their backs. When they rattle their quills the noise warns other animals to keep away. The quills are hollow so they make a loud noise.

Death-watch beetles live inside tunnels that they have made in wood. They send messages to each other by banging their heads on the tunnel walls.

Beavers slap the surface of the water with their flat tails to warn each other of danger.

Rabbits thump their feet on the ground when danger is near. This warns other rabbits of the danger.

Rattlesnakes have a rattle on their tail. They shake this rattle when a dangerous animal comes too close.

Male grasshoppers communicate by making a chirruping sound. They do this by rubbing their rough legs against the edges of their hard wings.

There are about 10,000 different kinds of grasshopper and each type has its own chirruping sound.

People living in parts of Africa sometimes use drums to send messages. The sound of the drums can travel a long way.

Try this

Try using a drum to send messages to a friend in another room.

First, you will need to work out together the different drum beats that you will use for different messages. Two beats could mean "Can you hear me?" Three slow beats could mean "Come here."

Movement and shape

People often communicate by moving their hands and arms.

Many animals also send messages by moving parts of their bodies.

A male fiddler crab has one claw that is much bigger than the other. It uses this big claw to send signals by waving it in different ways.

One type of signal warns other males to keep away from its burrow. Another signal attracts female fiddler crabs.

← These birds are great-crested grebes. They have crests on their heads, which they raise to show that they are looking for a mate.

16

Some animals can change their shape when they are in danger.

When a toad is threatened by a grass snake, the toad stands on tiptoe to make itself look bigger – too big for a grass snake to eat in one gulp.

Frilled lizards live in Australia. When they are threatened, they raise the frill around their neck, which makes them look larger and more frightening.

The head of an elephant hawk-moth caterpillar swells up when it is frightened. This makes the coloured spots on its head look like big, angry eyes.

When a porcupine fish is in danger, it suddenly puffs itself up with water.

17

Some animals communicate certain things by making movements that look very like a dance.

Honey-bees visit flowers to collect pollen and nectar as food. When a honey-bee that has found food returns to its hive, it makes waggling movements that look like a dance. This tells the other bees which way to go to find the flowers.

Japanese cranes are tall, graceful birds that dance when they are looking for a mate. They dance around in circles, leap into the air and bow to each other.

People use dances to communicate too. Sometimes the dance tells a story.

19

Smell

Some animals use smells, or scents, to communicate with each other.

Moths use scents to find each other in the darkness. Male moths have large antennae on their heads. They use their antennae in the same way that we use our noses.

A female moth sends out a scent that is carried on the wind. The male is attracted by this scent and follows it until he finds the female.

Ants lay a trail of scent so that they can find their way back to their nest.

Scents are often used as warning signals.

A greenfly sends out a warning scent when it is attacked by a ladybird. The other greenfly know that this scent means 'danger', so they drop off the plant and escape.

Light

A firefly is a kind of beetle that communicates by using flashes of light.

◀ The firefly has a small patch on its tail that can shine in the dark.

Female fireflies do not have wings. Their flashes of light tell the male fireflies which direction they must fly in to find them.

There are lots of different kinds of firefly. Each kind uses a different pattern of light flashes.

The firefly's flashing light is like a signal ▶ from a lighthouse. Each lighthouse along the coastline sends out a different pattern of flashing light. This helps sailors who are out at sea in the dark to check where they are.

Try this

In a darkened room, use a torch to send messages to your friends with flashes of light.

Again, before you start, you will need to work out what some of your signals will mean. You could use a different number of flashes to mean different things.

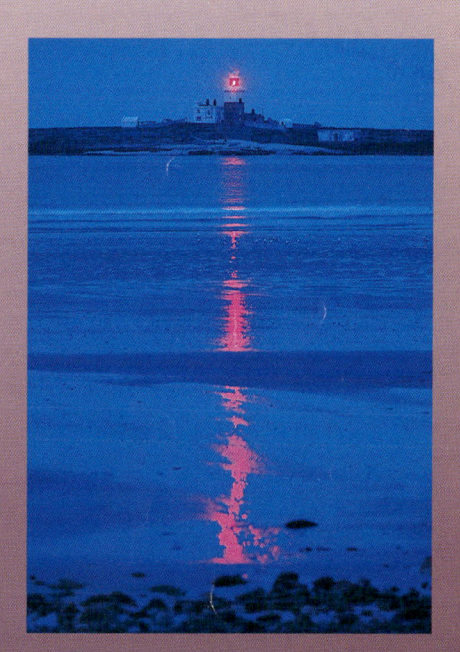

Use your head!

Animals chirrup, howl, puff themselves up and grow bright feathers to communicate. Humans talk, wave, smile and dress up. But humans can also invent other ways to communicate.

How do people communicate if . . .

. . . they cannot hear?

. . . they are underwater?

. . . it is very noisy?

Can you think of any more examples?

22

Glossary

attract — When an animal needs to find a partner (or mate), it usually has to do something special to get the other animal's attention, or to *attract* its mate.

crest — a tuft of feathers on the head of a bird

hover — Some birds can stay in the same position in the air for a long time. They *hover* by moving their wings very fast.

mate — Animals need to find a partner before they can produce young. An animal's partner is called its *mate*.

nectar — a sweet liquid produced by plants

pack — a group of animals that live or hunt together

pollen — a powder produced by plants. Bees carry *pollen* from one plant to another and this helps the plants to produce seeds.

scents — These are different kinds of smells made by animals or plants. Some smell nice and some smell horrible. Most animals can recognise more scents than we can.

shoal — a group of fish swimming together

23

Index of animals

ants 20

beavers 14
birds 6, 8, 13
　see also ducks, great-crested grebes, humming-birds, Japanese cranes, peacocks, robins
butterfly fish 9

caterpillars 17
cats 7
coral snakes 6

death-watch beetles 14
dogs 13
ducks 8

elephant hawk-moth caterpillars 17

fiddler crabs 16
fireflies 21
fish 9
　see also butterfly fish, porcupine fish, sticklebacks
frilled lizards 17
frogs 11, 13

grasshoppers 15
great-crested grebes 16
greenfly 20

honey-bees 18

humming-birds 9

Japanese cranes 19

ladybirds 10, 20
lizards 17

moths 20

peacocks 8
porcupine fish 17
porcupines 14

rabbits 14
rattlesnakes 15
robins 10

seals 12
skunks 6
snakes 6, 15
sticklebacks 10

toads 17

wasps 11
wolves 12

24